To My Generation

I0159554

C'Yana

***

ISBN-13: 978-0615736808
ISBN-10: 0615736807

***

To contact the author:

http://tomygeneration.blogspot.com/

***

Published by:
Keni Arts Int'l
www.keni.com

Table of Contents

Forward

Poetry is considered a form of communication-
language. God, the creator of all things, thought it
necessary to allow such a style of writing to be
written in the Bible. Solomon, former King of
Israel, the wisest man of his age, wrote many
poems in the book of Proverbs. These writings are
geared towards inspiration, motivation, and even
challenging the reader for change in ones mindset.

I find it such a delight, and with great joy to introduce
to you an anointed, yet talented, wise young lady,
"Miss. C'Yana …."

When I began to hear her recite her poems she truly
captivated my heart, as I know it will yours.

C'Yana has a desire to speak to others directly through
her writings so that they will be inspired,
encouraged and changed by not only her own life
experiences, but by Divine revelation of the Spirit
of God.

In 2012, C'Yana was asked to recite one of her poems
at a women's conference. She did not want to
share one that was already written. I joined her by
the pool-side at the hotel the evening before her
presentation. While I sat and enjoyed the serenity
of beautiful Palm Desert, she spent time listening
to the voice of God to give her what He would
have her to share.

To my surprise, within 30-45 minutes later, C'Yana asked me if I would read what the Lord had given her. As I read through her poem, without getting through half of it I had to stop and take a breath of air because I could not believe that in such a short time, she received such revelation and actually wrote it in poetic form. Not only that, but it was written to fit and relate directly with the flow of the message for the conference. As I had the opportunity to introduce her the next day at the Conference, little did I know that I would soon have the privilege and honor to introduce her to the world in her very first book. She has committed herself to reach the nations with her God-given gift.

As you read through her poems, understand that these are not just mere made up poems, but that they are strategically orchestrated by the Holy Spirit, spoken and written out of the mouth of such a young "Gifted Writer of Life"…Ms. C'Yana Edison-King.

Through her writings you will truly be mentally captivated, emotionally engaged, and surprisingly encouraged, as it brings solace to the soul.

It is said that "The Mind Is a Terrible Thing to Waste"…not so with this young gifted writer, instead she has allowed her mind to be used as a ***"MASTERPIECE"!***

Minister Rebecca D. Casey, PhD.

Acknowledgements

Not an ounce of this book can be said to be all of me.
So many people contributed to its success,
whether it be in a little way or a huge way.
First, I'd like to give my utmost thanks and praise to
my Father God, for it was His words written on
these pages, and by His will that it was published.
My family was some of my biggest supporters: my
mom, Shawneece Edison, and dad, Kawaun Wade,
my grandparents, Reggie and Beverly Monroe,
and my great grandparents, Pops and Grandma
Jones. They were there through thick and thin. I
thank you guys for all those late nights staying up
with me while I wrote, constantly reading and re-
reading poems, and for believing in me even when
I didn't believe in myself.
I thank God for bringing me to a church that actually
challenged me as a Christian, giving me the truth
with no sugar coating, and always giving me love
and support. A few of my poems have actually
come to mind as a result of the teachings of Pastor
Anthony and Dr. Micheline McFarland. I
appreciate those from the church who took the
time out to really influence my life; whether it be
constant words of encouragement, checking on
me, or supporting me.
A special thanks to a few people of the church such as,

Mother Ferguson, Dr. Sean Johnson, Ms. Gloria
Maxey, Doug Sparks, Ms. Debi Ellis, Mrs. Karis
Joseph, and of course my Publisher, Keni Arts
Int'l.

To my Godparents, Roland and Becky Casey, thank
you guys for the constant faith and love.

And thank you to all my true supportive family and
friends and anyone else not mentioned. Although
you may not be directly acknowledged, trust that
you are definitely appreciated and well
acknowledged in my heart.

I thank God for the people in my life, I don't know
where I'd be without them.

Introduction

After coming close to losing something, we often tend
to appreciate it a little more than we did before.
The value of one's life is probably the most often
taken for granted. However the value of God is the
most PRECIOUS thing taken for granted. You see,
life is a gift from God which makes it that more
special than the breaths we take. Yet we often
seem to spit in God's face with our back stabbing
decisions to hurt our bodies and turn from him.
However, despite whatever we are going through
the only thing we can do is live life and trust in
God. I wrote this book to express the value of
both. I write to express the importance of things
often unaddressed, to inform without lecturing,
and to hopefully reach someone when my words
are all they need to hear.
With life situations and God being the overall theme of
this book, the poems are relatable to almost any
generation. Yes the direct audience is indeed my
generation, the young teens of the world today, but
I write to speak to everyone.

Chance at Peace

Peace seems so impossible to obtain.
People stripping others of the very blood that flows
    through our veins.
The word peace isn't present in our dictionary, a word
    with a meaning you just don't comprehend.
A foreign language, a word like some fashion designs
    you just can't trend.
People killing one another.
Stories on the news, headlines reading:
    Boy who killed his own brother.
    A man set on fire.
    Person beat with a tire iron.
Kids committing suicide, due to bullies at school.
Seems like the world was based upon a different rule.
Treat others how you'd want to be treated must have
    gone out the window.
You wouldn't like being called names and being
    pushed around, trust me I know.
The Lord said "peace be still," but not an ounce of
    peace exists.
The church itself doesn't contain peace in it.
Violence and aggression the answer to every question.
No one paints their faces with smiles, the world lives
    in depression.
Everyone seems to wear an anger problem.
The problems presented in life, God can no longer

solve them,
At least that's what people think.
Foul words and putting people down is all that you can
    speak.
And yet people wonder why the world can't find peace.
You can't find peace in a place with people crushing
    each other's dreams.
Parents with kids they often strangle.
Treating them like bulls at rodeo you can wrangle.
People putting bullets in other people's chest.
Who gave you the right to put someone in a permanent
    rest,
The right to mentally abuse, the right to end one's life?
Who gives you the right?
Leaving a generation to grow up in hate.
Little girls growing accustomed to rape.
Young black men can't walk the streets at night.
A cop can take his life and still just walk away like its
    right.
There used to be a time when you can leave your gate
    open and your doors unlocked.
Try that now and I guarantee you get popped.
A world of change is my only will.
A world where finally, peace is still.

Hell and Back

Fade to black, thinking about my past as I look back.

All I see is shame and pain.

Earthly things instead of Godly dreams.

Drugs and alcohol, yeah I did it all.

Now I can only shake my head, for His forgiveness I'd
always beg.

For I knew of grace He was, but then I'd go and make
Him hate He was.

Making the devil grin as I went and dished out his
work of sin.

Pulling people down instead of uplifting them.

Switching my side of the team.

Dealing with greed and hate, switch up change, then

I'm back to heavenly things.

Wishy-washy Christian, playing both sides of the
fence, being oh so fake.

In church praising His name, then 12 o'clock came; off
to the streets to disgrace His name.

It wasn't like I meant to do it, but it became like a habit
I got use to it.

I'd try to change and live my life right.

Put up my fist and against the devil I'd fight.

But the constant pain caused me to lose faith, made it
hard to walk His path straight.

I drank and did drugs to fill the void.

I did all of the devil and none of the Lord.

It felt so great; those few minutes of high lifted me up
    and let me forget about life.
In the fast lane going the wrong way.
Speeding towards fire instead of something so much
    higher.
And although it was like I'd never truly try,
I got the hint when I almost lost my life.

Make it Right

Down on my knees, hands up, head down.

Found myself saying the same prayer I've said so many times.

Like a skipping disk, constantly on replay.

Asking God to forgive and forget the mistakes that I made.

Put my sins in a cup, trust it'll over flow.

But my gracious Father always lets it go.

Seemed like so many times I'd go and please the devil.

Putting myself in so much trouble.

Then on Sunday when church came, I'm on the alter crying out God's name.

Claimed to be a Christian, when I wasn't being Christ like.

Doing things I knew just weren't right.

Knowing in my heart I'm causing pain to my Father God.

While the devil sits back, kicks his feet up and applauds.

Putting smiles on the wrong face.

Causing my fate to head to the wrong place.

Change of direction.

And it seemed as if nothing would cause me to make the correction.

Like a magician playing tricks.

Making people think I was so sweet, when I was just
  being slick.
I could recite the Ten Commandments like they were
  written on my hand.
Can turn you from sin, and lead you to salvation right
  where we stand.
And even through all that, it wasn't like it truly
  mattered.
It was like my sense of right and wrong was
  completely battered.
It took a night when I should have lost my life.
To finally realize I need to make things right.
So here I am for the last time.
Down on my knees, hands up, head down.
Only in this case I'm here to talk to God about
  something so profound.
I'm here to ask Him one last time to forgive me for my
  shame.
And to truthfully from this point on live in His name.
To be an honest Christian, being Christ-like.
Doing all and only what's right.
I realized not everyone gets that chance to turn their
  life around.
So I better take my chance now, before I'm taken off
  this ground.

Y.O.L.O.
You Only Live Once

Silent killer, quick and steady.
Sometimes slow but always ready.
Painful oh no, it'll take you in your sleep.
So carefully done you can't even hear it as it creeps.
Not a crack will squeal.
It's hard to believe this killer is even real.
The thing that's always so funny is that you invite him
    into your home.
Through your hallways it has roamed.
Held its hand.
Claimed it to be your special friend.
Facebook shows evidence of your little friendship.
Pictures with captions saying look what I did.
Introduced it to your other friends.
So cool it became a new trend.
You're sitting here looking puzzled but you know what
    I'm talking about.
He's the reason why your own house you were kicked
    out of.
The reason why you were expelled from school.
But also the reason why your friends think you're so
    cool.
You know that blunt and bottle you had in your hand
    while you danced.
Remember that party you went to that the cops
    crashed?

I know you couldn't have forgotten you were taken to
the police station.
Because they said you were so intoxicated.
Oh, well there's a chance you might have forgot.
That's one of your little friends' gifts, erasing
memories and removing thoughts.
Let me state a little fact; throw something to your ears.
Your little friend kills fourteen hundred teens a year.
Do you think you'll still be cool, when you're buried
six feet under?
When your Mom can only toss and turn in the covers.
Teen's party, get drunk and high all the time.
I guess that's part of the reason why we're dropping
like flies.
Yeah sure it makes you feel good, you forget about the
problems of life.
But would you still do it given the chance you could
die that night.
Because you are.
Sure you only live once that's the new teen theme
Y.O.L.O.
But why purposely cut that one life short, you know?
Am I the only one that gets this?
Am I the only one willing to reject it?
I guess maybe it's something you just have to see for
yourself.
But by the time you finally get it, it'll be too late to
save yourself.
When you're standing in front of God and the question
why is asked.

You'll think back to when that drink went around the
    circle and you'll wish you would have passed.
Your motto for life would no longer be Y.O.L.O.
    because the truth about drugs… you'll finally
know.

Puzzles

Trying to put together the pieces to the puzzle.
Trying to figure out the reason why my family
    struggles.
Is it my sins finally catching up; the fact I lived a life
    so corrupt?
I asked for forgiveness I tried to change, but constant
    repetition maybe the cause of my pain.
But as I sit here fighting to solve this puzzle.
I realize that the struggle was the cause of most of my
    troubles.
I was born, raised, and lived in the church.
To the devil I was a threat, a disease, or some curse.
Through the little problems my faith stayed strong.
I knew if I kept my mind and heart on God not a thing
    could go wrong.
So the devil started throwing hard balls and I began to
    strike out.
I showed strength on the outside, but inside I was
    freaking out.
Contemplating on if I could survive through this
    attack.
When I felt like I couldn't handle it I began to draw
    back.
But the fight wasn't over, the bell hadn't rung.
I still knew I was here because of God and His Son.

The devil took this with envy and began to attack me
  mentally.
Out of fear I broke away from God completely.
I paid no attention to a man named God and all He had
  done for me.
Church was a mere word in my dictionary.
And even though I often attended, I felt like I was out
  here on my own like I was in solitary.
I was falling like a deck of cards in a pyramid.
Despite my departure from God, in which I thought
  was the solution, my problems were still so
  myriad.
A constant attack, it seemed so infinite.
I started to realize that God wasn't the cause of it.
I had a recollection of these things called trials.
And in those trials my faith in God is something so
  vital.
The importance of me being able to put my problems
  in His hands and trust He'll solve them.
Instead of playing on a one-man-team expecting to
  win.
So as I was holding the pieces, cramming my brain
  trying to figure this puzzle.
I threw my struggles to the ground, walked away
  saying Lord I leave you to handle my troubles.

Live or Die

You say for your child you'd give your life.
In your beating heart you'd stick a knife.
But with a gun pointed at your head would you still
    believe what the Bible said?
Would you deny Jesus Christ if that's all it took for you
    to live your life?
Crying out Lord forgive them, would you declaim?
Could you still praise Him and uplift His name?
Would you still walk through church doors if you knew
    you'd face deadly horrors?
You breathe each breath knowing God's the one
    pumping blood through your chest.
Saying your prayers each and every day, thanking God
    for always making a way.
The thief comes to steal, kill and destroy.
But the Power of God you always deploy.
In faith you stay strong when everything has gone
    wrong.
But will you still speak His word if at your neck lays a
    sword.
Will the name Lord God still flee your lips, if you
    knew you'd be burned with sticks?
Could you still sing and dance, lift up your hands.
Walking the streets teaching of God, sharing His good
    deeds.
Not of this earth simply a visitor since birth.

You stand in church, shout amen at the things the
    preacher says.
Doer of His word and not a hearer alone.
Claiming God's promises as your own.
Do you believe in your Heavenly Father, whom you
    cannot see?
Rather than the man your peers praise on TV?
You say you're a child of God, not of humanity.
You live for a man who lived for you, but would you
    die for the man that died for you?

Smile in the Rain

Some people ask why I always smile so brightly;
Why a frown is never present on my face, not even
    slightly.
They wonder why I walk around so proud.
Stand so tall I almost touch the clouds.
How I seem to point out the bright sun on a cloudy
    day.
How I can find color in something so gray.
I say you have to find the little bit of sun shining
    through the rain.
Realize the joy, look past the pain.
Forgive and forget about the wrongs done to you.
Use the hurt to fuel everything you do.
Don't let the little things dry out your tears.
Grab hold of the Power of God and overcome your
    fears.
Realize you're probably not living the worst life.
Now I'm not trying to turn your gallon of struggles into
    a pint.
I'm just trying to give you something to smile about.
Give you that silver lining in the dark clouds.
If our lives were depressed off every little thing,
No one would ever reach their dreams.
Appreciate the tiny specs of blessings you receive each
    and every day.

And remember even though you're out in the world
    filled with pain,
Someone got stripped of their life today.
God never said each day our heart will beat, and on
    this earth we'll forever breathe.
Often, in times, we take advantage of the things we
    need most,
because they seem to just be a given.
God never promised us life on earth or hearing.
So I just thank Him for giving me life despite my
    wrong decisions.
I kind of like to think of it as a privilege.

Inspiration

Inspiration, an act or quality that influences or arouses
the mind, creative imagination, or emotions,
something so inspired, as an idea.
Inspiration, something to fuel every last thing you
think of.
A spec of something that gets the gears in your mind
grinding.
It gives you that oomph and energy to keep you
striving.
Inspiration, something so magnificent.
A process so crazy you can't explain it.
Like a light bulb lighting up above your head.
That spark that hits your mind and the idea just
spreads.
The pieces to a puzzle found and solved.
One thought totally evolved.
Inspiration, that plug to new creations.
A whole new movement.
An automatic connection you can't even prevent.
Inspiration, that thing that makes your mind wild out of
control.
Fast feet, fast hands, your actions speeding towards a
new goal.
Like it's from another source.
It may change your life, switch up your course.
Inspiration, a spark of influence.

Whether you hear it, see it, or have a thought wrapped
through it.
Something that flashes and triggers a part in the brain
to create an idea something so insane.
A wild thought yet so beautiful.
To your mind it's so fruitful.
Something so automatic and uncontrollable it's like
temptation.
Inspiration.

Lead Way

Step back, let Him take the lead.
Switch roles, passenger seat.
Let Him ride out, while you just follow.
Put your problems into His hands, let go of all your
    troubles.
Clear your mind and don't stress.
Take a deep breath; let it flow through your chest.
With the Father God on your side, you never have to
    worry.
Everything against you will scurry.
All that you need will be taken care of in time.
Your special moment shall soon shine.
The devil can get you when you're really not trying to
    be got.
But when God is at the wheel, the devil will be
    stopped.
Don't let your ego make you think you're in control.
Let the Holy Spirit play His role.

Words of Music

Metaphors of sex and drugs flow through the
  headphone wires.
Hip hop only, never a church choir.
Pastor preaches about the wrong it does to your spirit.
Then you say you'll stop, you begin to fear it.
But then you go and put the headphone right back in
  your ear.
Knowing what's coming out of it, you really shouldn't
  hear.
But because you're so use to it you act like you don't
  even care.
Partial guilt of wanting to be accepted.
Friends' laughing because your iPod is pure gospel is
  always expected.
Lust and disrespecting women seems to always be a
  lyric.
But it just doesn't faze you, like you don't even hear it.
The beats addicting, it gets you mesmerized.
Plays tricks on you, does things to your mind.
Makes you think that it's okay.
But tell me ladies, why it's good to be called a name
  any day?
Slowly dissecting at the morality of good.
Take away all that was instilled in you, yes it could.
Break down the word of God eventually.
And the crazy thing is it could all happen subliminally.

Mind Control

Sitting in front of a screen.
Staring at such a scene.
Almost like being drawn in.
Attracted to something so capturing.
Trying to turn away but it's grabbed your attention.
With a tight grip it has you pulled in.
What you're seeing may not be so good.
Watching something you don't think you should.
And even though you're trying to block it out.
With your brain it has a direct route.
Like a USB connected to an iPod and computer.
Press sync and the information becomes a fast
    commuter.
Brain washed and hypnotized.
I'm talking about something big, a subject so
    magnified.
Subliminal changes to the mind.
An issue with a direct problem you just can't find.
Sudden change, crazy thoughts.
All based from some things you shouldn't have heard
    and shouldn't have watched.
Constantly seeing blood being splattered as an ax is
    thrown.
Then you come to find blood is all you seem to know.
You hear rappers saying money and cars make you so
    tight.

Now you're sitting here thinking it's the new way of
life.
Violence and aggression are now your answer to every
question.
How about God, that's my new suggestion.
Look in the mirror and find a new person.
Almost like what you're seeing isn't your own
reflection.
Like what you've seen didn't affect your eyes.
And what you heard couldn't affect your ears even if it
tried.
Instead of in one ear and out the other, it headed up the
brain in one big cluster.
Subliminal changes to the mind.
An issue with a direct problem you don't THINK you'll
ever find.
But you'll come to find the answer if you just hit
rewind.

What Skin Am I

What skin am I?
Is it black or white?
Is it dumb or smart?
Is it pain and sorrow?
Many may say that a black woman's color is the shade
of her past.
A dumb, gold digging, black woman that couldn't play
a part in this world.
But to me it doesn't matter what they say.
So I ask again, what skin am I?
I am a young, educated, talented black woman.
I try hard in this world and don't take anything for
granted.
I work hard to fulfill my dreams.
God made me and I am proud to say I'm His child.
I love my Father and value my body which is His
temple.
I live my life strutting my stuff because I know who I
am.
I uphold the scars of a black woman's past.
I feel the pain and happiness, the earth and heaven.
I understand that the world has changed,
only it hasn't seen the truth.
My color has no connection to my knowledge!
I am strong. I am intelligent; I can play my part in this
world.
Yes my skin is black, but my blood is red!!!

My Woman of God

Strong and virtuous.
Loves so openly like it's a must.
The roots of the family tree, what holds it all together.
Despite what wrongs we do she'll love us the same
    forever.
Blooming like a beautiful flower.
Growing more and more with God's power.
Smart and intelligent.
Hard as nails yet oh so delicate.
Problem solver.
Heart reviver.
The one to put the smiles on our faces, when we can
    only frown.
There to pick us up every single time we go down.
Took us to church each and every Sunday.
Her answer to every problem is to get on your knees
    and pray.
She's the glue to hold us all together, the rock to hold
    us down.
The woman to keep our world moving round.
The peacemaker, the stress taker.
She's the woman of our world, and I hope she knows
    we appreciate her.
I love you Mother.

Toast to a Grand Father

A girl's father holds a special place in her heart.
A place of love and peace in which no one can break
    apart.
From day one the love seems to just be a given, that
    first moment she looks into his eyes it's almost
    like she sees Heaven.
The angel sent from God to be her special lover and
    protector.
To heal and prevent any wounds from anyone trying to
    hurt her.
The one to pick her up as she cries from horrible
    dreams at night.
He sits her in his chest, kisses her and hugs her tight.
Someone who buys and teaches her how to ride her
    first bike.
The man who checks for monsters in the closet and
    flicks on the nightlight.
He scares away boys who claim they want to play.
Picks her up from school each and every day.
Dusts off her knees when she falls down and tries to
    warn her about no-good-boys who come around.
And when she gets older and her heart is broken.
He'll find that boy and pay him a visit with words
    unspoken.
He's that man you see in the stands with a camera at
    every event.

Every sport, concert, recital, and pageant.

Do his best to be there for her no matter what's needed.

A shoulder to cry on, a good laugh, or a hug if that be
it.

A long talk about whatever she'd like to get off her
chest.

She thinks about her father, knowing she's truly
blessed.

From day one he's been there and she prays to God
he'll be there till the end.

She hates thinking about losing him because she knows
that will be the day her world will end.

I know this because I too love my father beyond the
stars.

My love stretches out for him high and far.

My father's a star player and I'm his number one fan.

The only difference is my father has a prefix reading
Grand.

A Divine Destiny

Called for a purpose by my Father God.
Headed towards success our calling is not a façade.
Called to touch the world and minister to its people,
To make an impact that only He knows.
To be a blessing to someone's life,
And help set them on the path that's right.
Strong and wise,
Yet something so precious in His eyes.
So special that even God Himself took His time.
The extension of Him, made in His image.
To live on this earth and fulfill His vision.
We are all here for a different purpose,
To do whatever God may asks of us.
Sent to be in someone's life for maybe only a season,
But even in that short season we are there for a reason.
We as His daughters have callings to fulfill.
For us to be successful is His only will.
Predetermined greatness,
Something you can't replace.
Here to fulfill our destiny,
To try and keep anyone we can from the enemy.
We are Daughters with a Divine Destiny.

Friendship

A friendship is a relationship like no other.
It's almost as strong as one between a sister and
brother.
They stand together through thick and thin, and when
against the world they always win.
Well not truly always.
Sometimes the world comes with those rough days.
Those go home and turn your pillow to a river, tough
days.
The ones when you wish the whole world didn't even
exists.
Or at least a time machine because in a heartbeat you'd
flick that switch.
As quick as melting butter on a skillet you'd turn back
the past.
But those lessons in life you'd definitely grasp.
The heartache you caused yourself, yet alone the one
you caused others.
Especially the one caused to someone you once called
sister or brother.
A friendship can't take all the weight of the pain the
world caused, because we're only human.
But then again, it wasn't the world's fault you fell into
it.
Yet what's a strong relationship without having gone
through troubles.

To My Generation

How do you really know life if you haven't had to
    struggle.
It takes tough skin and God to make it through.
To learn those lessons only life can teach you.
Because every friendship starts with a
    "I'd never change", "I'd never hurt you",
    "or a boy/girl will never come between us two".
But even Justin Bieber told us never say never.
But in all honesty people are stubborn and think life
    lessons are better.
Hey maybe they are, those are the ones that stick.
Like being sprayed by a skunk a heavy fowl stench.
In the end "I'm sorry" is all you can say.
But you know you're mind is speaking more,
you can't even get it all out in a single day.

Your Definition of Love

Crushed heart and a confused mind.
All from a love I just knew was mine.
But oh how much wronger could I have possibly been.
When love itself is now followed by sin.
The word love once used for what it truly meant, now-
a-days it's used to get what you want.
Guys say they love her but it's just a front.
You love what her body looks like and what it makes
you do.
Rather than the beautiful feelings she sends your heart
through.
Boys and girls have changed the definition of a word
once so sacred.
Love was never easy but now it's pure hatred.
Love isn't purposely causing pain.
Making the one who truly loves you shed a tear for you
every day.
Wishing, hoping, and waiting for the day you'll finally
see,
That the girl you're with isn't half as good for you as
she.
Deep inside she knows her love for you is her ultimate
rival.
But despite the pain she's in complete denial.
Hoping and praying that you'll soon come to your
senses.

She waits with still patience.
But while you're trying to figure it out or when you
    finally see what was going on,
She'll be way past you, long gone.
In the end the fault will be on you,
Because you spoke to other girls with the head beneath
    you.
You played with the word love and hadn't truly meant
    it.
Or maybe you did but you sure didn't show it.
You yourself set you two apart, because you weren't
    true to your own heart.

C'Yana

Life for a Life

This past week I celebrated my seventeenth birthday.
While my aunt celebrated her son's when she went to
 his grave.
My cousin was four years old when he was put into the
 ground.
Although it was hard, we had to face that he'd no
 longer be around.
I could never grasps the reason why God could take a
 life so young.
Regain the life of innocence rather than one of a drunk.
I couldn't understand why so much sin still deserved
 the right to live.
While a spirit was taken out of the body of a kid.
Churchy people would say we we're all given an
 assignment.
But no one told me how so much wrong could possibly
 do it.
I'd sit and wonder why he died but I was still alive.
I was caught up in the drugs and i ran the streets with
 guys that popped slugs.
In my mind I was worthless, but according to the
 people of my church I had a purpose.
How could God give someone, doing the opposite of
 his will, something to fulfill?
To me it just didn't make sense. But then again no life
 is worth more and no life is worth less.

We all reside on this Earth for a reason.

And we live our lives by the seasons.

Sometimes it takes someone to go through trash to
realize what they had.

Sometimes they turn to God after a world of bad.

It's not God taking a life because of their wrongs.

It's them fulfilling what was needed then him bringing
them home.

It's not a matter of right and wrong, good or bad.

It's simply God taking back what he once had.

Instead of looking at it like they were stripped of their
spirit.

Think of them taken to a place of peace to live in.

Our sins aren't what causes us to lose our life.

Forgiveness of our sins is why on the cross Jesus died.

If our wrongs determined how much less our lives
were worth, then wouldn't Jesus still walk this
Earth?

C'Yana

Wake Up

We sit in church wide awake, but our minds are sound
asleep.
We sit here so unconscious, but our souls are trying to
speak.
It's screaming at us shouting to us, but we just aren't
listening.
But it's a shame because it's telling us everything we
need.
It's telling us to wake up; it's time for us to get ready.
It's not to long before the Savior is coming.
It's telling us to unplug from this world it's time to
renew our minds.
But our minds are thinking what do you mean, This
world is just fine.
We pay little attention to the sins we see daily.
Almost like we think this is how it's supposed to be.
Like it's fine to be cross dressers and dikes.
And a woman kissing a woman is all right.
We let MTV teach us morals, and Desperate House
Wives teach us values.
It's like you think the Bible can't teach you something
you can actually use.
We've become accustomed to the fad.
Ladies thinking it's cute to show the lower part of your
back.

Letting men degrade you, just because he says he loves
  you.
But God has a love that won't actually hurt you.
We live in sin throughout the week and hit the club on
  Saturday.
Then on Sunday you're at the altar trying to pray.
You cry to God, forgive me, I'm trying to change.
Oops, now look at what you're doing the next day.
You get all scared and depressed.
You've realized you do the things the pastor preaches
  against.
Your spirit is trying to prep you and get your mind
  right.
But your mind is sleep, and the sleep feels nice.
Your spirit is trying to tell you something...
    IT'S TIME TO WAKE UP!

Spiritual Father

Many people are confused on the actual meaning of a
    father.
A father isn't simply the man that married your mother.
Yet alone the man whose blood flows through your
    veins.
A father is a man who's there for you each and
    everyday.
Whether he's there physically or just a phone call away.
The one that helped to make you the person you are
    today.
A man of God who took you in as his own child.
Even when you wanted to act wild.
The man who'd give his life for you.
He told you he'd always be there, and he's proven it to
    be true.
This one goes out to all the fathers.
Whether you're a biological father, a family friend,
    grandpa, uncle or even a big brother.
The ones who tried their best to make sure you know
    your great.
The ones who told you your looks aren't your only
    trait.
The guy that told the little girls they're beautiful inside
    and out.
The man who was there for you without a doubt.

Present during those good times and even there for the
bad.
Who tried his best to make you smile because he hated
to see you sad.
The one who refused to let you become anything less
than what even you yourself thought you could be.
He told you that life isn't limited to what seems to be
Reality, and that you could one day live your
dreams.
This goes out to the man who lifted you up and
brought you to God.
Even when others thought it wasn't truly his job.
The guy who made you look beyond the stars and feel
like you're on top of the world.
He made you feel like you're his only girl.
The one who raised you to be a "Woman of God".
Never afraid to spare the rod.
This goes out to you!
To let you know we truly appreciate all you do.
And even if your blood doesn't flow through our veins;
or on our birth certificate isn't signed your name.
We want you to know that you are our father and we
sure do love you!
I would like you to know that you deserve a
Happy Fathers Day too!
So Happy Fathers Day to all of you!

Because of the Blood

Heart broken,
Pain stricken,
Shoulders holding a cloak of pain.
Tears of disappointment flowing like rain.
Your brain stuck in that one mistake.
Focused on the act in which you can never retake.
All those people that lifted you up you let them down.
And you didn't just drop them you punched them to the ground.
The feeling of no longer being worthy.
The love they had for you is now gone surely.
If you only had a bag to throw over head.
To cover up that shame and all the tears you shed.
These are thoughts that flow through your mind.
Forgiveness?
Please there is no kind.
You beat yourself up inside for the wrongs you've committed.
For the fact that your conscience said this is wrong but you dismissed it.
Heavy heart you hold deep within.
You can't even forgive yourself for your own sin.
You think everyone will judge you like they have their own court.
But in reality they have their own list of sins in which to sort.

Jesus said thou without sin cast the first stone.
And with that being said not one stone will be thrown.
Not a soul on earth lives without flaws.
Your family loves you despite the pain you may cause.
And when all else fails there's someone whose love
    will never end.
No matter what you may do it will never rend.
A love that is stronger than the strongest bone in the
    human body.
If you think I'm joking I just need you to trust me.
When the world turns its face from you.
God will still be true.
With Him forgiveness is real.
And it's not something you're forced to steal.
Repentance and a turn from sin is all that's needed.
For this Jesus was hung on the cross and for our
    forgiveness he pleaded.
He shed His blood to pay for our sins.
So that when we're down in the game we can come
    back and win.
When you feel like the world is holding your wrongs
    against you.
Remember Jesus died for your forgiveness and that is
    one thing that's true.

Cover Design & Art

www.ingramcontent.com/pod-product-compliance
Lightning Source LLC
Chambersburg PA
CBHW060627030426
42337CB00018B/3242